An Imminent Threat to Marine Ecology

Ballast Water Management System to Save Marine Life

Sunil Sarangi, MS, MBA

Independently Published
Printed in the United States of America, First Edition 2019

Table of Contents

Preface

A significant research activity has occurred in the area of global discharge standards of ballast water. Many countries have tried to come up with a treatment system that is fit for purpose and low maintenance costs. Despite the numerous contributions, there still exists a lack of knowledge of the issue and threats this ballast water discharge causes.

Today the possibilities seem immense, with new approaches to treat the ballast water during the discharge. Almost all stakeholders: Government, Shipping Industry, Academia and people wanting to see the invasive species completely eradicated.

Although, my book is intended mainly for mariners and vessel owners, I hope it will be useful for anyone that is interested to learn about a new subject of invasive species and its immense effect on our oceans.

For the past 12 years, I have worked as an Engineer / Project Manager for ballast water treatment companies in the USA, where I have made it my mission to deliver a quality product to the ship owners/Shipyards. Dedicated to continuing professional development, my credentials include a Bachelors in Marine engineering, Masters in Ocean engineering and MBA in project management. I have delivered 40 plus ballast water treatment systems to vessel owners till date.

"The best way to become acquainted with a subject is to write a book about it" Benjamin Disraeli. I wrote this book as an overview of ballast water and its management for the shipping community. I hope this book will be a valuable reference for researchers and engineers.

Sunil Sarangi - Oct 2019

***

Acknowledgments

I would like to express my sincere gratitude and thank all my friends. I worked with many good people throughout my career and they have taught me a lot and I learnt a lot from them, I express my sincere gratitude and I thank them all.

I wish to express my sincere gratitude to those who have contributed to my life and to my works anonymously. I thank all those who helped me a lot in preparing this book.

Introduction to the Ballast Water

International Trade - exporting and importing products locally and internationally has been a huge part of the trading system that benefits the economy of the country and businesses nowadays. The economy's progress has increased exponentially with the advent of marine trade that enables people to exchange goods and services from one place to another. As time went by, the concept of trading developed more, for the past few decades.

For the trading to be successful, cargo ships are commonly used in transactions where it exquisite goods from one country and exports it for distribution in other areas or to another country. When cargo ship travels, it is already loaded with cargo. But if it discharges load, it no longer carries any weight. In turn, the ship's stability is affected. This is why cargo ships require ballasting or carrying tons of water to ensure their safe operations. And when it reached its point, the water is being dumped in the lake. This water is called the 'ballast water' that serves as the compensation for different cargo loads that ships can carry everywhere, anything during loading and unloading.

However, in recent research proposed, it is said that one out of four threats in marine biodiversity is the destruction or reduction of the natural habitat and ballast water does impose a serious threat to the aquatic ecosystem and to the environment as a whole. How so?

The process of loading and unloading ballast water imposed a serious threat to the marine environment, biodiversity, economy and even public health as it imports fouling-species and invasive aquatic species or the "silent killers" such as the round goby, spiny water, zebra and quake mussels. They invade other aquatic habitats and successfully take their oxygen and food.

According to the National Invasive Species Information Center (NISIC), invasive species could be the plants, animals, microbes or pathogens that are non-native, exotic species or alien to a specific ecosystem which likely to cause harm. These foreign aquatic species could also diminish other ecological species that impose another problem.

Approximately 10 billion tons of ballast water are transported each year and an estimated 7000 species are spread to new habitats every hour. There is about 1 new invasion every 9 weeks. An interspecific competition becomes more intense with the native species and has a huge impact on the native ecosystems.

Many international agencies such as a specialized agency of the United Nations, the International Maritime Organization (IMO) proposed solutions for the responsible safety and security of the cargo ships preventing marine pollution.

Everything should all about prevention - clean, drain, and dry.

History of Ballast Water

In the middle Dutch and Scandinavian origin, the word "ballast," means "useless load". As the demand for global shipping increases, cargo ships are required to use ballast to operate successfully and be manoeuvrable in compensating the absence of cargo.

After several decades later, a German Scientist carried out a survey while he was getting a sample of flora and fauna at the Suez Canal. A Plankton Scientists later realized that the ocean water used for cleaning purposes on board contained microscopic organisms. They might've realized that these unwanted species survived the pumping activity of the water pumped on board to fill the ballast tanks.

Not until 1973, the issue about Ballast water impacting economic, ecological, and public health issues has been a concern and different ecological and marine agencies reviewed the problem in detail. Resolution 18 of the International Conference on Marine Pollution recognized the issue. The World Health Organization (WHO) along with IMO passed a resolution referring to the Research about the effect of discharge of ballast water containing bacteria of epidemic diseases.

The Invasive Species whether aquatic or not are the result of millennia of co-evolution by organisms adapting to the environment of one are to another. If the limiting factors of a habitat fail to stop the growth of species, then it would multiply, out-competing native species, bringing billions of dollars and irreparable change and damage to biodiversity.

In the late 1980s and early 1990s, Canada and Australia brought their problems in invasive species to the IMO's Marine Environment Protection Committee where some IMO members presented a case study research and argued international organizations to rule on this issue.

In order to prevent the negative effects of ballast water, cooperation and collaboration among government, non-government, and international organizations along with economic sectors happened. The IMO has been the lead or the front face organization that addresses the transfer of invasive aquatic species (IAS) through cargo shipping.

In 1991, the Marine Environmental Protection Committee (MEPC) adopted a resolution entitled "International Guidelines for Preventing the Introduction of Unwanted Aquatic Organisms and Pathogens from Ships' Ballast Water species and Sediment Discharges".

Its aim is to provide guidelines on the procedures that will minimize the risk of inviting unwanted aquatic organisms and pathogens caused by ballast water. Several factors were first checked before the implementation such as the types of organisms targeted, level of risks involved, environmental risks, and economic and ecological expenses involved.

Within this Guideline, the Port State Authorities allows the use of ballast water with appropriate Ballast Water Management Practices that are aimed to prevent and minimize contamination in water or ballasting and DE ballasting operations. Port State Authorities sets conditions and practices to comply with this purpose. The conditions include appropriate ballast water management plans, proper training for the ships' crew and officers, and the nomination of key control personnel.

The proper training for the ships' crew and administration should involve awareness of the ecological and health hazards posed by the loading and unloading of ballast water and maintaining tanks and equipment free from sediment. On the other hand, the

United Nations Conference on Environment and Development (UNCED) that was held in Rio de Janeiro in 1992 recognized the issue as a major international concern.

The 18th session of the IMO Assembly in 1993 adopted a resolution A.774 (18) based on the 1991 guidelines requesting the MEPC and MSC to research their studies in order to further develop internationally applicable legal provisions. The ICES WGITMO also emphasizes the need to follow this resolution. This year as well, it was also suggested to exchange ballast water to the seawater to minimize the risks of biodiversity and economic hazards.

Other Multilateral Environmental Agency (MEAs) such as the United Nations Convention on the Law of the Sea (UNCLOS) and the Convention on Biological Diversity (CBD) support IMO's effort in prevention, managing, and controlling alien species.

In 2004, the International Convention for the Control and Management of Ships' Ballast Water and Sediments and also known as the Ballast Water Management Convention (BWMC) is the framework instrument with the aim of addressing the threats imposed by ballast water and the IAS. It was eventually adopted by the IMO Diplomatic Conference in February. IMO assembly revised Resolution A.868 (20) and adopted it as a convention.

There are given two options in replacement of ballast water:

1.   Emptying the whole tank and filling it and;

2.   Not emptying the tank but proceeding to the filling by allowing the overflow to come out by the air outflow in which could be three times the volume of the tank that has to be exchanged.

The Ballast Water Cycle

The four-process in Ballast Water Cycle or Ballasting:

1. At the Source Port
From here, there are no cargo load yet and the ballast water must provide a load for the ship to trim, maneuver, and for stability.

2. During the Voyage
There are no cargo load but the ballast tanks must be full with ballast water.

3. At the Destination Port
New cargo is loaded while the ballast tanks are discharging the ballast water.

4. On the Return Trip
The ship is loaded with cargo but there are no ballast water inside the ballast tanks.

In other terms:

Unloading Cargo - Loading Ballast Water

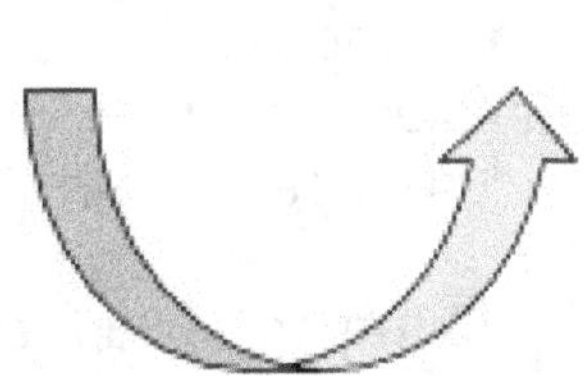

Voyage - No Cargo, Ballast
Voyage - With cargo, No Ballast

Full Tanks

Infographic 1: Ballast Water Cycle
Loading Cargo - Discharging Ballast Water

When ballast water is taken on board, this means that there is no cargo inside the ship. But if the cargo is loaded with the shipment necessary, the ballast is discharged from the ship.

Ballast Water Management Convention

After more than 14 years of complex negotiations between IMO and different and international Marine Agencies, the International Convention for the Control and Management of Ships' Ballast Water and Sediments (BWM Convention) was later on adopted by a general agreement at a Diplomatic Conference in IMO Headquarters in London on 13 February 2004.

The Total Enterprise Value (TEV) risks is about US$90.4 billion based on its resources in fisheries, marine reserves, biodiversity, and tourism. However, the overall potential costs were estimated due to the lack of data. The costs implementation of BWM Convention in the country is around US$5.6 billion. The cost of implementing the BWM Convention in Chile is estimated to be around US$5.6 billion.

In conclusion, even if there is a little effect from the

IAS introduction, economic loss is still greater than the BWM implementation. It is best to ratify and implement the BWM Convention as an important mechanism to control the IAS.

The Main Requirements of the Convention:
- All ships allowed and permitted are required to have a ballast water management plan and a ballast water record book on board.
- All Ballast Water and Sediment Management need to be carried out in all voyages without exception.

It is necessary for the ships registered in BWM Convention to carry the following:
- Ballast Water Management Plan (BWMP) - It includes all the ballast water's detailed description of all the actions, practices and requirements to be taken in the implementation when conducting ballast water exchange. It also provides safety measures, guidance, and assistance to the vessel's crew and operators to avoid operational delays which can help to save time and money.

The following are the Details that the BWMP should include:
- Shore facilities and locations where vessels should load and unload cargo and ballast water.
- The list of Rules and Regulations provided and according to the International law about different Port State Control.
- The operational procedure of the Ship when ballasting and deballasting.
- The Necessary conditions in carrying out a ballast operation.
- Limitations and Restriction of the exchange
- The Duties of each crew member while the ship is carrying out ballasting or de-ballasting.

- The given sampling and treatment method for ballast water.
- Sampling Points of Ballast Water.
- The Plan necessary for the Ballast Water Tank
- An Updated and Accurate Log Keeping
- Ballast water Record Book - to record any exchange of ballast water from loading to unloading. This record that could be in physical or electronic form is a part of the critical success in the management plan that gives proper and accurate documentation of how successful (or failure) the exchange was.

The representative listing of the book must include the:

1. The longitude or latitude location where the ballast water exchange occurs.
2. The detailed position both of the watertight and weathertight closure after the exchange happened.
3. The accurate descriptions of the procedures when conducting ballast water exchange.

Authorized Port State Officers are the only ones allowed to inspect the record book and they were able to determine whether to make a copy of the entries or not as long as it has a permit in any legal proceedings as evidence of facts.

- International Ballast Water Management Certificate - issued on behalf of the Administration or Flag States that certifies the ship in carrying out ballast water management in accordance with the BWM Convention. This certificate specifies which Standard (D-1 or D-2) is the ship complying and its expiration date.

The BWM Convention obliged all ships to implement a proper ballast water management plan and carry out ballast water management procedures in a given standard. The factors included are the ballast water treatment equipment, control, and monitoring equipment, piping arrangements, and sampling facilities.

Based on Lloyds Register Marine, staff must be trained with the operations on board, maintenance of the system and proper measures with the ballasting operations or treatment system. The International Chamber of Shipping and Resolution MEPC.300 (72) that was adopted on April 13, 2019, provides detailed information about the Ballast Water Management.

The 18th session of the IMO Assembly in 1993 adopted a resolution A.774 (18) based on the 1991 guidelines requesting the MEPC and MSC to research their studies in order to further develop internationally applicable legal provisions. The ICES WGITMO also emphasizes the need to follow this resolution. This year as well, it was also suggested to exchange ballast water to the seawater to minimize the risks of biodiversity and economic hazards.

In 2017, all ships must have an approved Ballast Water Management Plan onboard, a suggested Ballast Water record book for tracking purposes, a to be surveyed and issues by an International Ballast Water Certificate by IRS. It's an utmost importance for the ship's master, officers, crew, and staff to have a full and proper understanding of the ballast water management in order for it to be carried out effectively and efficiently.

Ballast Water Management System Code (BWMS Code)

This code is aimed for Administrations and their designated offices, bodies or agencies to assess the BWMS in meeting the standard regulation D-2 of the BWM Convention. It would also serve as a reference for the manufacturers and ship owners on the evaluation procedure that their ships need to follow according to 'the Convention'.

The BWM Code provides two primary regulations with the intention to reduce the invitation for the invasive species: "Regulation D-1, Ballast Water Exchange" and "Regulation D-2, Ballast Water Treatment."

1. **Regulation D-1** plans to reduce invasive species by unloading them before even arriving at the different port at least 200m in depth and 200 nautical miles offshore. In coastal voyage, at least 50 nautical miles away from the nearest port; Exchange Standard. This regulation is only applicable to all the vessels that were built before the implementation of the convention.

2. **Regulation D-2** plans to remove invasive species at specified levels prior to discharge by developing several new shipboard systems. These systems are yet to be approved by the IMO; Performance Standard. This regulation is applicable to all the vessels that were built after the entry into force of the Convention.

Regulation D-3 also requires that ballast water management systems to use Active Substances (G9) that consists of a two-tier process - the Basic and Final Approval in ensuring that the BWMS does not pose more risk to the environment, biodiversity, public health, and to any other property or resources.

Additional Regulation D-4- Prototype Ballast Water Treatment technologies stated that the technologies used for the Ballast Water Treatment must be tested with five years duration while the Regulation D-5 - Review of Standards by the Organization must review the standard regulations of the Convention to ensure a safe and environmentally friendly ballast water discharge.

Negative Effects of the Ballast Water

The IAS transported from the ballast water cannot be stopped by any predators or diseases to limit their population growth as they outcompete the native species by preying on them or taking over their habitat space and food sources.

Ecological Effects

Once the non-native species are discharged to a certain water body and if it can manage to survive and reproduce, they can become a product of plague to the environment.

Risks include the chemical waste, loss of native biodiversity due to the destruction of the food web were the non-native species are preying or competing with the native species. Non-native species also smother, overgrow, causing genetic dilution, and worst, extinct in where it can lead to the decreasing rate of habitat availability and would result in them, risking their lives.

Environmental Effects

This includes the changes in the environmental nutrient cycles in exchanging necessary air, air pollution, and processes and decreasing water quality that can lead to negative results on shipping cargo in coastal areas, fishing, and availability of drinking water.

Effects to Human Health

As the human race is linked to bodies of land and waters, a single change to the ecosystem can bring a major effect on people. Toxic, Bacterias and Foul-odored smell that IAS brings and spread to the environment can affect us greatly. These would affect the way we eat, our foods, and provoking health problems might arise.

Risks also include decreasing recreational and leisure activities, overgrowth of aquifers or underground layers of rock saturated in water, suffocating water bodies, and an increasing number of parasites and disease.

Economic Impact

Economic impacts from the IAS can damage food production and the industry itself. It can also interfere with the fisheries, destruction of the tourist spots, damaging infrastructure, energy consumption, and biological resources that support the fish and coastal aquaculture. Moreover, the country's financial system is affected when there is a need for the money used to use in preventing and eliminating invasive species.

Invasive Aquatic Species (IAS)

A healthy ecosystem is maintained by a balance through different limiting and environmental factors such as geography, food availability, presence and absence of predators, nature, and thereof. A sudden visit from an Invasive species would bring major change. Regardless of where they came from, how they arrive, and where would their new expected homes would be, they still put the economy, environment, public health, and ecosystems at risk!

The Invasive Species whether aquatic or not are the result of millennia of co-evolution by organisms adapting to the environment of one are to another. If the limiting factors of a habitat fail to stop the growth of species, then it would multiply, out-competing native species, bringing billions of dollars and irreparable change and damage to biodiversity.

Invasive Aquatic Species affects public health (both for humans and animals), the economy, and the environment by disrupting the food web essential to every living organism, deterioration of natural habitat, dominance towards the native species, a decline in fisheries, and some epidemic diseases.

IMO GloBallast provided the top 10 Major Invasive Aquatic Species (IAS) that everyone should be aware of and here are 5 on the list:

Infographic 2: DYN Lionfish

Lionfish (Pterosis)

Lionfish, also known as the "Hoover vacuums of the sea", are originally from the Indo-Pacific and was first introduced off the coast of South Florida in the mid-1980s. It has twelve different species and all are adorned by its beautiful bold maroon, brown, and white stripes that feast on shrimp and smaller fish. Since then, it became one of the most prolific invasive aquatic animals in the world.

Lionfish has a fast-growing breeding rates that can consume up to 460,000 prey fish per acre over the course of one year (a single female can produce about 2 million eggs per year). They also have a huge appetite that can expand up to 30 times their normal size.

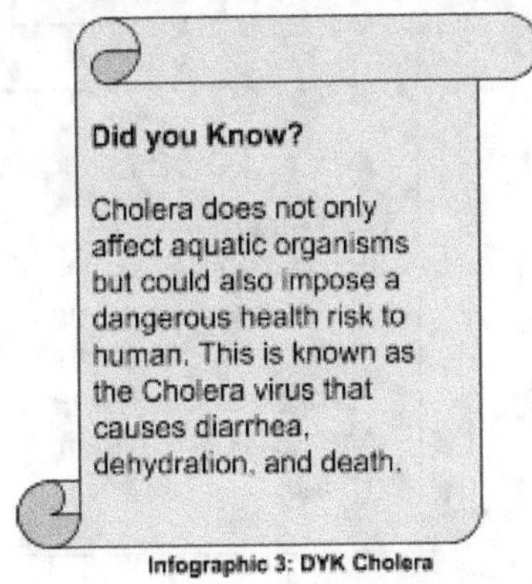

Infographic 3: DYK Cholera

Vibrio Cholera (Various Strains)

This type of aquatic species that are commonly carried by ballast water is an intestinal infection. It is native various strain with broad rangers that were introduced majorly to South America and the Gulf of Mexico.

Vibrio Cholerae is a gram-negative, comma-shaped bacterium where the natural habitat is brackish water or saltwater. It can cause mild or severe results to organisms affected. In severity, it may cause death this is why it is sometimes called 'blue death' and was introduced to the Baltic Sea.

Cladoceran Water Flea (Cercopagis Pengoi)

The Cladocera a small Crustaceans, which is commonly known as the water fleas were originally known as Black and Caspian Seas. Its body has flat-disks shaped and not segmented. Three parts can be distinguished: head, thorax, and abdomen.

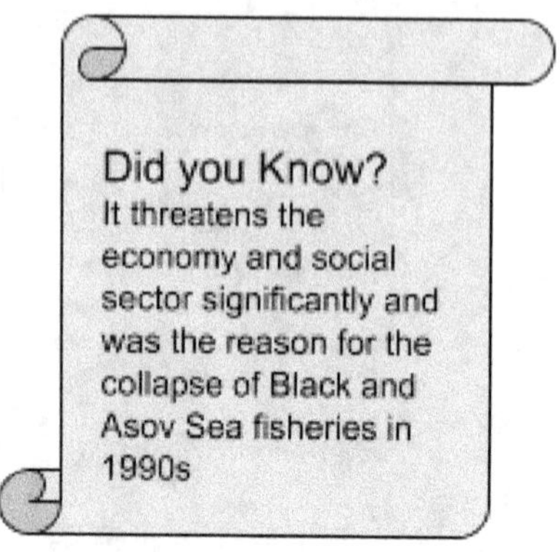

Infographic 4: DYK Comb Jelly

Over 650 species have now been recognized and some of its species grow from 0.2 mm up to 5 mm although most of it rarely exceeds 3mm. It can reproduce both sexually and asexually resulting in large populations that dominate the zooplankton community and clog fishing nets and trawls.

North American comb jelly (*Mnemiopsis leidyi*)

This not-so-friendly comb jelly were natives of Eastern Seaboard of the Americas and was introduced to Black, Azov and Caspian Seas in 1982.

It has an oval-shaped body and is transparent with four ciliated combs and tentacles. It reproduces rapidly depending on the condition. It feeds and depletes which alters the food web and ecosystem functions.

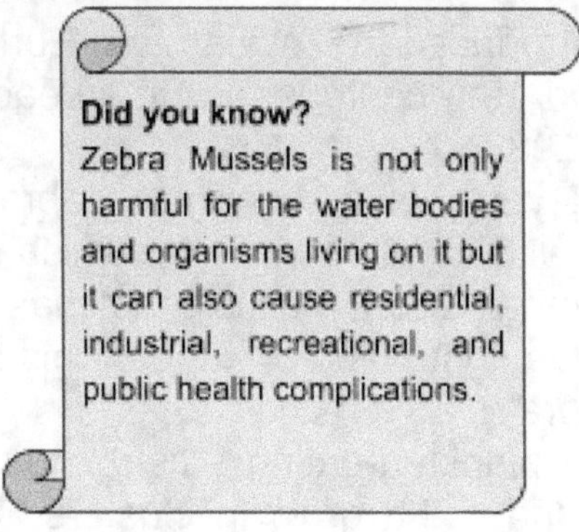

Infographics 6: DYK Zebra Mussels

Green Crab (Carcinus maenas)

This common type of littoral crab has been carried by the ballast water from the European and African coasts.

This typical looking crab that could grow 6 to 10 cm has a shell or carapace that is broad, serrated and has a trapeze shape with 5 acuminate yellow anterolateral teeth and eight eyes in total. It has various colors usually dark brown, dark green, red, and yellow granules depending on physiological and ecological differences based on its origin.

It can live from four to seven years and can release 185,000 eggs once or twice a year. It can affect a native ecosystem and organism as it is a predator on bivalves, worms, mollusks, shellfish, and other crustaceans making it one of the worst, if not the worst, clam predators we know" based on MacPhail and his contemporaries.

Zebra Mussel (Dreissena polymorpha)

Zebra Mussels, considered the most dangerous invasive aquatic species, are originally from the Eurasia seas such as Black, Caspian, Aral and Azov seas. They were first introduced to Russian and European canals in the 18th and 19th centuries but it spread through North America in 1988.

At first, you would recognize zebra mussels as a small clam with a yellowish or brownish shell. However, it is a fingernail-sized mollusk that has shells in color dark with little light-colored stripes. This is also why it is called a 'zebra'.

These plankton-eating fish has a massive population and could grow in clusters. They also have an aggressive growth that could lead up to two inches long. They're harmful because they filter out algae that the native species considered as food. The removal of these algae or phytoplankton can cause a shift in the food web disrupting the ecological balance. It also contains a high concentration of toxic materials that spreads within the lakes killing fish and wildlife.

BALLAST WATER TANKS

As stated by a Marine Engineer, a particular ballast tank is filled depending on the fixed position of the cargo load. This means that if more cargo load is located at the port side (left side) than the shipboard side (right side), then the port side of the ballast tanks are filled more of ballast water to gain overall stability.

Other factors to be considered when filling ballast tank are the draft required by the vessel, depth at the port, capacity, etc.

In the late 1980s and early 1990s, Canada and Australia brought their problems in invasive species to the IMO's Marine Environment Protection Committee where some IMO members presented a case study research and argued international organizations to rule on this issue.

In order to prevent the negative effects of ballast water, cooperation and collaboration among government, non-government, and international organizations along with economic sectors happened. The IMO has been the lead or the front face organization that addresses the transfer of invasive aquatic species (IAS) through cargo shipping.

The most common location for the ballast tanks on the ship is on the topside tanks, lower hopper tanks, double bottom tanks (db tanks), and Fore and Aft Peak Ballast Tanks.

Topside Tanks

The Topside Tanks has a triangular shape with wings on both sides of the cargo holds and said to help avoiding a shift in inaccessible spaces. These are more common in bulk carrier ships and are constructed using transverse frames.

NANPCA established an intergovernmental organization called the Aquatic nuisance species task force (ANS task force) to prevent the introduction of IAS and to closely monitor and study the species. A violation of the following regulations set by NANPCA may lead to civil and criminal penalties.

Although there are many successful implementations of this act, there are few setbacks that were found such as its inadequacy. This primary legislation is limited only within the Great Lakes area. As this act expired in 2002, Congress reorganized and reauthorized a new act called "National Aquatic Invasive Species Act of 2005" which was not yet implemented. It revised some of NANPCA's legislation in order to address the problem among the rest of the States in America. A few of its provisions was to regulate ballast discharge, prevent and control invasive species introductions, support management plans, authorize funds for state and regions, educate people about the ballast water, its risks, and laws. Again, non-compliance with these laws may result in penalties or fines.

It is directly connected to the ship's main ballast pipelines and helps in carrying cargo without the need for the trim.

Double Bottom (DB) Tanks

The double bottom of the ship is located between the forward part or collision bulkhead and after peak bulkhead which divides the engine room. This double bottom feature is used to avoid the ingress of water in case of grounding or collision.

The design would largely depend upon the length of the ship. For ie, when the ship is longer than 120 meters then the arrangement of the DB tanks and sloped bulkheads of the wing tanks would consist of longitudinal framing while for the ships with less than 120 meters, the arrangement would be transverse framing.

BWM helps to maintain and preserve native aquatic life protecting them from non-native species. It helps in minimizing and eliminating risks associated with the introduction of IAS such as spreading bacteria's and unhealthy organisms within the territorial waters and disrupting the ecosystem and biodiversity as a whole. This also helps in decreasing the effects on fishing, sea farming, and deterioration to port facilities.

The lower hopper and double bottom tanks can serve as the fuel tanks while, correspondingly, the top side tanks are ballast. Double bottom and fuel oil tanks aren't connected to the ballast system to avoid any chance of contamination.

In some ships, the double bottom space is divided into three sections (instead of two) in order to provide a cofferdam in the center known as the `duct keel' which is used to carry pipework, ballast and bunker tank valves.

Fore and Aft Peak Ballast Tanks
These tanks are provided within the ship to perform precise trimming operations and hardly filled to avoid the free surface effect of the liquid. The valve used in these tanks is only remote control (hydraulic) valves.

The design is far different from other ballast tanks as it would depend on the bow and stern design of the vessel. It has an irregular shape and narrows at the bottom end due to its location.

Ballast Water Management System Treatment Methods

Advanced water treatment systems and technologies are implemented when exchanging ballast water. However, there are factors to be considered in choosing the most appropriate, safe, and legal systems approved by the IMO and the BWM Convention such as the space on-board, cost-effectiveness and efficiency, environmental-friendliness, and ease of the operation and installation for the crew.

The treatment system deals with the mechanical, physical, chemical or biological methods of killing and/or removing potentially harmful aquatic organisms within the ballast water. It is a treatment system that is less disruptive for ships to treat ballast water problems without delaying or interfering with cargo operations.

It has a 'Pallet System' that requires no filtration, toxic chemicals, and UV Irradiation. The system kills invasive aquatic microorganisms through pasteurization and deoxygenating which also provides less corrosion by injecting nitrogen. The System uses onboard excess energy that makes the operation cost low with no up gradation of power generators or pumps necessary. Installation is flexible enough to be installed into a new and existing vessel.

There are different methods proposed to the IMO, however, only one has been approved yet. Since Science tested that aquatic species from coastal waters won't be to survive if discharged in an open ocean due to the difference in water chemistry, temperature, and salinity, so does the aquatic species from the ocean water if discharged in coastal waters. This is why the Ballast Water Exchange (BWE) is necessary.

- Ballast Water Exchange
- The process involves exchanging or replacing the water in the ballast tanks that should be carried out at least 200 nautical miles from the shore of location and the water depth is 200 meters or more.
- The simplest and most convenient method for ballast water management is accompanied by three replacement techniques namely sequential method, flow-through method, and dilution method.

Three Different Methods of Ballast Water:

Sequential Method - the ballast tanks are emptied completely until there's no more to be pumped by the suction and stripped by educator systems. It is then refilled by fresh open-ocean or ballast water one tank at a time. A transitory period and proper planning are necessary to ensure the accuracy and safety of the method within the accepted criteria.

Flow-Through Method - pumping of open-ocean water into ballast tanks allowing it to overflow through available air vents. The additional water can be used in weather conditions. Research suggests that it is necessary to pump three times the tank capacity 95% effectiveness in eliminating IAS.

1 Pump = 63% exchange	2 Pumps = 86% exchange	3 Pumps = 95% exchange	4 Pumps = 98% exchange

Infographics 7: Equivalent Pump Exchange for Flow-through Method

Dilution Method - pumping water from the top or opening of ballast tanks and simultaneously discharging the water to the bottom part. At least three times the volume of the tank is necessary to be pumped.

There are different types of water treatment methodologies and technologies available in the market primarily the:

- ***Mechanical Treatment Method***
- A method of filtering ballast water before it enters the tanks and departs from the origin port and from the port of another location.
- enables the organisms to be filtered out and possibly, retain their natural habitat without having an adverse impact on the marine environment.
- processes include filtration, cyclonic separation, and electro-mechanical separation.

Filtration	removing particles with disk and screen filters
Cyclonic Separation	allows particles to get separated from water due to centrifugal force
Electro-me chanical Separation	separate organisms, sediments, and water then filtered out.

- ***Physical Treatment Method***
- Method of Physical Disinfection by heating the ballast water from 35°C to 45°C in order to kill large organisms. It is heated by an engine cooling system without any resulting chemical by-products.
- processes include UV light, cavitation or ultrasound, and deoxygenation.

UV Light	Attacking organisms completely and prevent their reproduction
Cavitation or Ultrasound	Killing cells of organisms
Deoxygenation	Removing oxygen in tanks for organisms to be asphyxiated

- ***Chemical Treatment Method***
- A method in using chemicals to be shipped on board with proper safety procedures to be considered.
- Processes include disinfecting biocides and electrolytic chlorination.

Disinfecting Biocides	Uses disinfectants to kill organisms in the water and interferes with reproductive and metabolic system.
Electrolytic Chlorination	Running electric current to the water that kills organisms and generation of chlorine to disinfect.

INTERNATIONAL LEGISLATIVE OF IMO

Each country in the world has its own legislative frameworks depending on the local constitutional structure, national practices, laws, policies, and culture. However, there is one common goal - to create a safe practice for ballast water without providing any risks for the environment, economy, public health, and marine organisms and ecosystem.

Below are a few examples of countries with laws and policies approved and related to IAS:
The United Nations (UN) held a conference back In 1992 in Rio de Janeiro in Brazil which was called the "United Nations conference on environment and development". International maritime organization (IMO) proposed voluntary guidelines and developed a ballast water management convention and several other regulations. These regulations worked hard in finding measures in preventing and controlling the rapid spread of invasive species.

United States
The United States of America created federal laws, executive orders, and even state regulations to control the effects of ballast water within US waters.

Clean Water Act.
The first federal law in the United States regarding water pollution is the Federal water pollution control amendments of 1972 or most commonly known as the "Clean water act (CWA)", was administered by the Environment Protection Authority (EPA). However, controversies arise when CWA allows the distribution of water pollutants within the coastal area of the US if

permitted by EPA through the National pollutant discharge elimination system (NPDES).

Even if the ballast water plays a huge role in disrupting coastal waters, EPA considered it as a part of normal vessel operation and does not restrict nor requires a permit for it. Several environmental groups petitioned for EPA to repeal its exemption towards ballast water. Later on, through congress, the exemptions were annulled last February 6, 2009, requiring NPDES permits for vessels discharging ballast water pollutants to the US Waters.

Executive Order.

President Clinton signed Executive Order 13112 in 1991 for federal cooperation towards the growing problem of IAS. The main goal is to prevent and control the escape or release of unwanted species into a new coastal ecosystem.

EO issued a National invasive species management plan that would the specific objectives, goals, and measures that were carried out by the Federal Agency. The implementation of the plan should be developed through a public process where there is a consultation from the agencies and stakeholders.

National Invasive Species Act

The Senate and House of Representatives in the United States also assembled an act called the Nonindigenous Aquatic Nuisance and Prevention and Control Act of 1990 (NANPCA) to prevent and control invasive organisms within the coastal areas of the country.

Studies have shown the difference between the ocean and coastal waters where the former does not carry many harmful organisms. Even if it does, it cannot survive in the coastal environment. The NANPCA requires all vessels entering and leaving United States territory to carry out its exchange beyond the exclusive economic zone (EEZ) or on the high seas and exchange the ballast water from other waters where it does not pose a threat in infesting and spreading IAS. The other option is to use environmentally sound alternative ballast water management methods that are found to be as effective.

NANPCA established an intergovernmental organization called the Aquatic nuisance species task force (ANS task force) to prevent the introduction of IAS and to closely monitor and study the species. A violation of the following regulations set by NANPCA may lead to civil and criminal penalties.

Although there are many successful implementations of this act, there are few setbacks that were found such as its inadequacy. This primary legislation is limited only within the Great Lakes area. As this act expired in 2002, Congress reorganized and reauthorized a new act called "National Aquatic Invasive Species Act of 2005" which was not yet implemented. It revised some of NANPCA's legislation in order to address the problem among the rest of the States in America. A few of its provisions was to regulate ballast discharge, prevent and control invasive species introductions, support management plans, authorize funds for state and regions, educate people about the ballast water, its risks, and laws. Again, non-compliance with these laws may result in penalties or fines.

As stated by a Marine Engineer, a particular ballast tank is filled depending on the fixed position of the cargo load. This means that if more cargo load is located at the port side (left side) than the shipboard side (right side), then the port side of the ballast tanks are filled more of ballast water to gain overall stability.

Other factors to be considered when filling ballast tank are the draft required by the vessel, depth at the port, capacity, etc.

There are three states that passed the mandatory ballast water exchange and management laws namely Washington, California, and Michigan.

Australia and New Zealand Coast

In Australia, ballast water brought about two-hundred invasive aquatic species and has been introduced to their coastal waters. Few of these species are the toxic dinoflagellate, Northern Pacific Seastar, Asian Kelp, and Giant Tube Worm that brought major harmful impacts towards the local marine ecosystem.

Along with Australia is New Zealand who were the first two countries who filed an international appeal for the invasive aquatic species introduced by ballast water. In New Zealand, about one hundred and fifty invasive marine species have been introduced which was only fifty thousand less than those in Australia. The two most common species found are the Algal Bloom and Undaria Pinnatifida.

Legislation, Regulations, and Programs.

In order to reduce the risks caused by the invasive species into the Australian coastal waters through ballast water, the Australian Government implemented requirements in July 2001. These requirements were applied through the Quarantine Act of 1908 and are operated by a federal government agency, Australian Quarantine, and Inspection Service (AQIS).

AQIS is a government agency that has the responsibility of ensuring that there are no high-risk foreign ballast water or any other import that would unload inside Australia's territorial sea before permitting foreign ships to enter. It uses x-ray machines and sniffer dogs in searching for a quarantine risk material.

The Australian Government also developed a comprehensive national approach known as the National System for the Prevention and Management of Marine Pest Incursions (the National System). This includes a National Monitoring Strategy (NMS) to monitor species with significant impact and locations that can be easily invaded.

The Objectives of The National System is to

a. Prevent the translocation of non-native species to Australian Sea Territories.
b. A ready-response team is provided in case an outbreak of non-native species happened.
c. Control and Prevent the rapid increase of non-native species.

The three major components of the National System:

1. Prevention Systems that helps to decrease the risk of introducing and translocation of IAS.
2. Emergency response to the new IAS in eliminating and reducing them within the coastal territory and;
3. Managing or controlling already found invasive species in Australia.183 It also has several others.

New Zealand implemented regulations to control and minimize the discharge of IAS within its coastal waters. The rules states:

- All ships voyaging to NZ should avoid unnecessary discharge of ballast water not unless it is for the safety and stability of the ship.

- If the ship was loaded from another country besides NZ, it is not allowed to discharge within the country without permission.
- Only NZ Quarantine Officer will grant permission for the discharge.
- Every ship voyaging to NZ should record volume, location, and date where the ballast water was loaded.
- Ships are only required to exchange load ballast water in mid-ocean using a refill or flow-through method.

Even with the agencies and rules provided by both countries, there is no case law available in dealing with ballast water.

United Kingdom (UK)

The half of invasive species found in the UK comes from the ballast water. But according to a study undertaken, the effects of these invasive species in the UK's coastal territory are not as detrimental as other parts of the world. However, few species such as Spartina alterniflora (Spartina),Sargassum muticum, and Coscinodiscus Wailesii.

Legislation, Regulations and Programmes the United Kingdom

As of today, there has been no legislation nor regulation provided by the Government and agencies in the United Kingdom that directly tackles Ballast Water discharge and its effects. However, the UK has been a part of various conventions that deal with the introduction of non-native species such as:

- Convention on Biological Diversity - June 5,

1992
- Bonn Convention for the Conservation of Migratory Species of Wild Animal
- Berne Convention on the Conservation of European Wildlife and Natural

The Act has 4 parts with 74 sections and 17 schedules:

Part I: **Wildlife** (Sections 1 to 27)

Part II: **Nature Conservation, Countryside & National Parks** (Sections 28 to 52)

Part III: **Public Rights of Way** (Sections 53 to 66)

Part IV**: Miscellaneous & General Sections** (67 to 74)

Operational Options:

Recommendation vi. Ballast Water should not be loaded or unloaded in non-native species' locations.

Recommendation viii. Risk Assessment Procedure States have to be developed.

Recommendation xviii. Only a preferred and suitable area should a ship traveling from one port to another should perform the ballast water exchange.

Recommendation xx. Ballast Water Exchange should be performed 200 nautical miles away from the shoreline and 200 m in depth.

Recommendation xxi. If ships were not able to perform ballast water according to the distance preferred, they should perform suitable ballast water management measures instead.

Recommendation xxii. All ships operating in a bio-province

Northwest European should be subject to a risk

assessment.

Recommendation xxiii. All ships within the UK or about to voyage to the country should have suitable management measures.

International Ballast Water Management Systems are also implemented in the countries included in the United Nations such as Canada, Brazil, Antarctica, and several others from South Africa and Asia.

Ballast Water Discharge Standards (per country)

The ballast problem also has an impact on other countries who uses cargo ships for trading. As the 'Global Ballast Water Management Project', was successful, IMO executed the United Nations Development Program (UNDP), the Global Environment Facility (GEF), and IMO or the GEF-UNDP-IMO GloBallast Partnership Programme to unitedly worked together in assisting developing countries with the reduction of IAS carried by ballast ships and to prepare the countries included for the implementation of Ballast Water Management Convention and act accordingly to the requirements.

The first phase that lasted for four years (2000-2004) assisted six developing countries namely Brazil, China, India, Islamic Republic of Iran, South Africa, and Ukraine carrying out effective measures with the introduction to foreign aquatic species. They were able to gain success in developing an international regulatory framework with their goal and was adopted by the IMO Member States of the BWM Convention.

The second phase, on the other hand, was able to use the tools and experience from the first phase in projecting its mission to 15 Lead Partnering Countries (LPCs) which are Argentina, Bahamas, Chile, Colombia, Croatia, Egypt, Ghana, Jamaica, Jordan, Nigeria, Panama, Trinidad and Tobago, Turkey, Venezuela and Yemen that also supports activities for more than 70 Partnering Countries (PCs).

According to IMO, the intervention in the LPCs had the following objectives:

- To expand the capacities of both government and port management
- To initiate the legal policy and institutional reforms at the national level
- To develop establish legal, policy and institutional reforms at the national level
- To develop mechanisms for economic and port sustainability and;
- To encourage regional coordination and cooperation
- Some services provided by the company are the: Information & Telecommunication Systems, Electronic Systems and Equipment, Smart life and Eco-friendly systems, and many more.
- This typical looking crab that could grow 6 to 10 cm has a shell or carapace that is broad, serrated and has a trapeze shape with 5 acuminate yellow anterolateral teeth and eight eyes in total. It has various colors usually dark brown, dark green, red, and yellow granules depending on physiological and ecological

differences based on its origin.

- It can live from four to seven years and can release 185,000 eggs once or twice a year. It can affect a native ecosystem and organism as it is a predator on bivalves, worms, mollusks, shellfish, and other crustaceans making it one of the worst, if not the worst, clam predators we know" based on MacPhail and his contemporaries.
- A method of filtering ballast water before it enters the tanks and departs from the origin port and from the port of another location.
- Enables the organisms to be filtered out and possibly, retain their natural habitat without having an adverse impact on the marine environment.
- Processes include filtration, cyclonic separation, and electro-mechanical separation.

Even though there are several countries joined hand-in-hand with the convention, these countries already experienced economic loss and health risks. It would be a challenge for the GloBallast to keep and to engage with the stockholders as they would be needing assistance to protect the marine environment from IAS. Without the stakeholders, it would be extremely difficult to encourage the IMO Member States in formalizing the program.

Partnering Countries and their Economic Assessment Rate:

Argentina

The National Economic Assessment (NEA) of Argentina was completed in 2012.

The Shipping industry plays an important role in the country's economic performance making 90% of the foreign trade based on maritime traffic. The trade balance in the fisheries sector has an average of US$1.15 million.

But the river, Río de la Plata has a 4,665 km long shoreline and navigable rivers and was introduced to thirty-nine new species with four of it being intentionally introduced to exploitation. Reports do not exactly state the cost estimation for enacting the BWM Convention for confidential purposes.

In conclusion, with the confidentiality of the exact figures and values on the technologies and potential costs in implementing the BWM Convention and introduction from IAS, a draft was still reported. Since the benefits of IAS prevention exceed the costs, the money, and the resources, it should be considered as an investment rather than a cost.

The Bahamas

The National Economic Assessment of the Bahamas was completed in June 2016.

The stakes of shipping in the Bahamas are high as it has one of the world's largest fleets with over 1.400 registered vessel and imports approximately 90% through sea shipping. Even though the country has a high vulnerability, it was not excused from the introduction of IAS. It affected the economic values of the resources such as fisheries, coastal tourism, and ecosystem services.

The overall economic value of resources at risk from the introduction of IAS was approximately US$1.6 billion per year. The cost estimation for implementing the BWM Convention was approximately US$1.7 million and US$110,000 annually and a range of US$5,000 to US$3 million per vessel (depending on its type and size).

In conclusion, the risk of the introduction from IAS exceeded the costs of implementing the BWM

Convention. Thus, it is best for the country to consider funding the development of BWM National Strategy to implement the BWM Convention.

Chile

The National Economic Assessment of Chile was finalized in January 2012. The country is vulnerable to IAS introduction risks as Chile has a long coast of about 6,435 km with high traffic volumes, geopolitical location, and export-based economy that relies on maritime transportation.

The Total Enterprise Value (TEV) risks is about US$90.4 billion based on its resources in fisheries, marine reserves, biodiversity, and tourism. However, the overall potential costs were estimated due to the lack of data. The costs implementation of BWM Convention in the country is around US$5.6 billion. The cost of implementing the BWM Convention in Chile are estimated to be around US$5.6 billion.

In conclusion, even if there is a little effect from the IAS introduction, economic loss is still greater than the BWM implementation. It is best to ratify and implement the BWM Convention as an important mechanism to control the IAS.

Colombia

The National Economic Assessment of Colombia was finalized in January 2011.

In conclusion, key economic sectors along with social and cultural impacts proposed a negative effect on the development of the country from the IAS Introduction. Thus, the NEA report suggested ratifying the BWM Convention.

Croatia

The National Economic Assessment of Croatia was finalized in September 2013.

There are six major ports which are Rijeka, Zadar, Šibenik, Split, Ploče, and Dubrovnik that are serving international trade in Croatia. The investment of these port infrastructure, shipping traffic, amount of ballast water, and the transportation capacities were increasing.

The estimated potential rate is not provided however if adding the potential costs from the IAS introduction risk based on TEV approach (US$2.8 billion) and implementation costs of BWM convention (US$1.4 million) along with the shipping industry (USS65.4 million) it would add up with an estimation of US$9.6 billion.

In conclusion, the implementation of the BWM Convention is relatively smaller to the negative effects of the introduction from IAS. Hence, it is feasible to implement BWM activities.

Egypt

The National Economic Assessment of Egypt was finalized in December 2011.

The IAS introduction could not only affect Egypt's fisheries, coastal tourism, and maritime transportation but it can also affect the main sources of income in the country. The major economic benefits of the country come from its marine habitats such as the Red Sea and resources like coral reefs, mangroves and seagrass beds that supply food, protect the shoreline, and secure economic benefits of the country.

The NEA dedicated a report to assess the economic values of Egypt that are at risk from IAS introduction based on the framework of TEV. It was conducted by applying market price analysis and travel cost method - two of the basic economic assessment method. The report provides details about the potential and existing resources at risk.

The report also mentioned that there are many parts of the marine ecosystem with no economic value since it has not been traded in the markets.

The overall potential cost of IAS introduction to the country is estimated to US$2.6 billion and the potential total cost of the implementation of the BWM Convention in Egypt is at US$4.5 million.

The same result from Croatia was concluded. IAS risk introduction cost was greater than the BWM Convention implementation. However, the actual values of resources at risk are likely to be significantly higher and considering values of other factors affected would lead the BWM Convention cost to decrease making it feasible to implement BWM activities.

Ghana

The National Economic Assessment of Croatia was finalized in 2011.

Ghana has a high risk of exposure to IAS as 85% of the country's international trade is carried by sea and is expected to rise further. In 2011, The Ministry of Fisheries reported that Ghana's fisheries sector contributes to the Gross Domestic Product (GDP) by 1.7% or approximately US$672.6 million. The economic value of coastal tourism was estimated at US$500 and the additional cost for conducting Port Biological Baseline Surveys (PBBS) was also reported. The BWM Convention implementation costs were estimated to US$183 million which is lower than the costs in IAS introduction risks.

In conclusion, the BWM Convention is economically feasible in implementing BWM activities as the relative costs were smaller than the potential costs of an IAS introduction.

Jamaica

The National Economic Assessment of Croatia was finalized in October 2016.

Even coral reefs alone are affected greatly by IAS introduction in the country that could cost US$23 per year and protecting it would cost US$9.9 million. But the NEA reported that Jamaica's Gross Domestic Product (GDP) has not been fully researched yet if the population growth of different organisms and resources in the country has not been properly checked, the Jamaican economy will lose more than of its total contribution to national GDP.

The NEA introduced two different cost groups for the BWM Convention cost - incurred in year 1 amounting to US$ 278,000 and recurring annual costs amounting to US$149,000 per year. In conclusion, the ballast water was considered the main cause of IAS introduction thus resolving a proper treatment for ballast water is a must. The BWM Convention can be implemented through sufficient financial resources allocation and ensuring their long-term availability.

The BWM Convention obliged all ships to implement a proper ballast water management plan and carry out ballast water management procedures in a given standard. The factors included are the ballast water treatment equipment, control, and monitoring equipment, piping arrangements, and sampling facilities.

Based on Lloyds Register Marine, staff must be trained with the operations on board, maintenance of the system and proper measures with the ballasting operations or treatment system. The International Chamber of Shipping and Resolution MEPC.300 (72) that was adopted on April 13, 2019, provides detailed information about the Ballast Water

Management.

In 2017, all ships must have an approved Ballast Water Management Plan onboard, a suggested Ballast Water record book for tracking purposes, a to be surveyed and issues by an International Ballast Water Certificate by IRS. It's an utmost importance for the ship's master, officers, crew, and staff to have a full and proper understanding of the ballast water management in order for it to be carried out effectively and efficiently.

Jordan

The National Economic Assessment of Jordan was finalized in January 2011.

The total cost of potential economic loss is estimated at US$811,000 while the implementation of the BWM Convention is approximately US$811,000.

Not until 1973, the issue about Ballast water impacting economic, ecological, and public health issues has been a concern and different ecological and marine agencies reviewed the problem in detail. Resolution 18 of the International Conference on Marine Pollution recognized the issue. The World Health Organization (WHO) along with IMO passed a resolution referring to the Research about the effect of discharge of ballast water containing bacteria of epidemic diseases.

In the late 1980s and early 1990s, Canada and Australia brought their problems in invasive species to the IMO's Marine Environment Protection Committee where some IMO members presented a case study research and argued international organizations to rule on this issue.

In order to prevent the negative effects of ballast water, cooperation and collaboration among government, non-government, and international organizations along with economic sectors happened. The IMO has been the lead or the front face organization that addresses the transfer of invasive aquatic species (IAS) through cargo shipping.

In conclusion, the BWM Convention implementation cost is feasible to implement BWM activities as it has a lower operational cost than the potential negative economic impacts of IAS.

Nigeria

The National Economic Assessment of Nigeria was finalized in 2011.

The NEA report assesses costs of economic values of resource at risks, potential costs from IAS introduction and BWM implementation costs that apply elements of the TEV-framework with market price and travel cost methods.

Based on the report from the Central Bank of Nigeria, the country's fisheries sector contributed to the country's GDP with 0.4% or approximately US$1.7 billion in 2011. The economic value of coastal tourism was approximately US$0.638billion and BWM Convention implementation costs to US$235 million.

Panama

The National Economic Assessment of Panama was finalized in 2016.

The country is vulnerable to IAS because the coastline is almost 3000 km long and it has the world's largest maritime fleet and high maritime traffic. Back in the year 1999, there was a recorded white spot syndrome virus and brought an economic impact of IAS when the shrimp farming was largely affected. The largest economic impact due to IAS happened.

An estimated cost of US$5.1 billion resources at risk and US55.8 million for the implementation of the BWM Convention. In 2016, Panama ratified BWM Convention and was recommended to develop the National Implementation Plan in the future.

In conclusion, as Panama was able to ratify the BWM convention already, it's safe to say that the result was feasible to BWM activities.

Trinidad and Tobago

The National Economic Assessment of Trinidad and Tobago was finalized in September 2013.

This dual-island Caribbean nation has a growing sector of the yachting industry and maritime shipping in accommodating the energy sector and facilitating trade between small islands and nearby countries. These sectors and the scale of oil tanker traffic and growing recreational vessels highlight the importance of dealing with IAS as a high priority.

Turkey

The National Economic Assessment of Turkey was finalized in 2010.

The NEA reported the negative economic impact of North American comb jelly to the Black Sea which was introduced by the ballast water. The report calculated total value estimates of key economic factors: Fisheries with USS1 billion, Aquaculture with US 323 million, and Coastal Tourism with US$18 billion. Other sectors were not available at that time of the report. The total potential costs of IAS introduction are calculated at US$8.16 billion while the BWM Convention implementation have amounted to US$822 million.

In conclusion, the BWM Convention is feasible to implement as the potential negative effects of IAS introduction was much greater. The NEA report also shows support for the national decision to ratify the BWM Convention.

Yemen

The National Economic Assessment of Yemen was finalized in November 2010.

There was still no adequate information nor database with information regarding the introduction of IAS in the country at that time but they prepared the estimated economic value of resources at risk using the formal statistical data available while the implementation of BWM Convention was based on training activities and work packages conducted by GloBallast Project in Yemen. The total BWM Convention implementation costs in Yemen are estimated at US$1.3 million.

The double bottom of the ship is located between the forward part or collision bulkhead and after peak bulkhead which divides the engine room. This double bottom feature is used to avoid the ingress of water in case of grounding or collision.

The design would largely depend upon the length of the ship. For ie, when the ship is longer than 120 meters then the arrangement of the DB tanks and sloped bulkheads of the wing tanks would consist of longitudinal framing while for the ships with less than 120 meters, the arrangement would be transverse framing.

BWM helps to maintain and preserve native aquatic life protecting them from non-native species. It helps in minimizing and eliminating risks associated with the introduction of IAS such as spreading bacterias and unhealthy organisms within the territorial waters and disrupting the ecosystem and biodiversity as a whole. This also helps in decreasing the effects on fishing, sea farming, and deterioration to port facilities.

The lower hopper and double bottom tanks can serve as the fuel tanks while, correspondingly, the top side tanks are ballast. Double bottom and fuel oil tanks aren't connected to the ballast system to avoid any chance of contamination.

In conclusion, the BWM Convention is feasible to implement as it outweighs the potential costs from IAS introduction especially if non-marketable ecological and environmental services, cultural values, and mitigative measures were expressed in monetary terms.

BWTS Treatment Systems Vendors List

A Marketing Research Firm, Technavio conducted a series of studies with the use of different technologies (Physical disinfection, chemical method, and mechanical method) and geography (Americas, APAC, EMEA) and was able to provide a market report that the global ballast water management market will grow CAGR 5% which could be equivalent to USD 2.7 billion from 2019 to 2023. And by the year 2021, the market is expected to grow with a Compound Annual Growth Rate (CAGR) of more than 31%. These organizations and companies that showed a proper intention to the market are vital to global trade.

Some factors that contribute to the growth of the market were the regulations provided by the IMO and their respective countries, the rapid growth of cruising leisure and business trading, shift in oil and gas operations for exploration and production, the introduction of IAS, and fleet size expansion in a global marine vessel.

The market report also analyzes the list of the market's competitive landscape and provided information on several market vendors especially the top five vendors in the market today:

ALFA LAVAL
- A Swedish company founded in 1883 by Gustaf de Laval and Oscar Lamm and created the Alfa Laval PureBallast BWTS that was approved by the IMO and USCG providing a total solution in ballast water treatment.
- A world leader in the market provides heat transfer, fluid handling, and separation. The company's system uses a UV reactor and filtration system in killing unwanted organisms.
- The company's products play an important role in power production, oil extraction, food manufacturing, and wastewater treatment.

GEA Group
- Manufactures from Germany and created the Ballast Master ultraV BWTS that was approved by IMO and Alternate Management System (AMS) from USCG. This ultraV BWTS is a highly efficient mechanical and physical system that is used for treating ballast water capacities and uses a 2-stages system mechanical pre-filtration and UV-C disinfection where no chemicals are used.
- The company is considered as the largest supplier of technology food processing and other process industries such as machineries, plants, etc.

Hitachi

- Hitachi is a global company with a Japanese origin from the Parent company, Hitachi Group that operates through diversified segments.
- It created the ClearBallast, a ballast water purification system that combines magnetic separation technology, coagulation, and magnetic separator to kill organisms such as plankton, bacteria, and algae. It was approved by the IMO since it does not use any chemicals.
- Some services provided by the company are the: Information & Telecommunication Systems, Electronic Systems and Equipment, Smart life and Eco-friendly systems, and many more.
- This typical looking crab that could grow 6 to 10 cm has a shell or carapace that is broad, serrated and has a trapeze shape with 5 acuminate yellow anterolateral teeth and eight eyes in total. It has various colors usually dark brown, dark green, red, and yellow granules depending on physiological and ecological differences based on its origin.
- It can live from four to seven years and can release 185,000 eggs once or twice a year. It can affect a native ecosystem and organism as it is a predator on bivalves, worms, mollusks, shellfish, and other crustaceans making it one of the worst, if not the worst, clam predators we know" based on MacPhail and his contemporaries.

Veolia Water Technologies (VWT)

- A water division company with a French origin from the parent company Veolia Group and considered to be the world's largest water services supplier.

- This company provides product and solution technologies that use disc filter and EctroSys disinfection unit. It is highly focused on different water treatments such as drinking water, wastewater treatment plants, process water, and bilge water treatment.
- It also offers a variety of services to cover water treatment plant management needs.

Wärtsilä

- A Finnish Corporate, Wärtsilä Oyj Abp or known by simply Wärtsilä manufactures products and services within the marine and energy market.
- It provides two BWTS to the marine market - Aquarius EC and Aquarius UV where the former uses filtration and electrochlorination and the latter uses filtration, UV irradiation without active substances in treating ballast water. Both of these are also IMO and USCG AMS approved.
- Few solutions and services it offers are ultra-flexible internal combustion engine power plants, utility-scale solar photovoltaic (PV) power plants, and liquefied natural gas (LNG) terminals, distribution systems, and marine oil and gas industry solutions.

The US Coast Guard Marine Safety Center provided a list of manufacturers who showed interest within the market and submitted a Letter of Intent (LOI) which is required by the regulations according to 46 Code of Federal Regulations Subpart 162.060-10(a). The LOI is prerogative of the vendors and necessary for the approval of their independent ballast water management treatment system.

Below is the list of twenty-four (not including the 5 names above) is approved by the Coast Guard:

Manufacturer	Date Received
BIO-UV	3/27/2015
Coldharbour Marine	5/28/2015
Desmi Ocean Guard A/S	2/7/2013
Eaton	3/12/2014
Ecochlor, Inc.	12/4/2014
ERMA First Esk Engineering Solutions	10/1/2014
Evoqua Water Technologies LLC	10/16/2014
Headway Technology Co., Ltd	8/13/2014
Hyde Marine	3/2/2015
JFE Engineering Corporation	11/18/2014
KSB Aktiengesellschaft	7/11/2014
NK Company Limited	5/11/2015
NEI Treatment Systems, LLC	2/6/2015

Oceansaver AS	12/17/2014
Optimarin AS	10/16/2014
Panasia Co..LTD.	12/9/2013
RWO GmbH, Marine Water Technology	6/26/2014
Samsung Heavy Industries Co., Ltd	6/24/2015
Severn Trent DeNora	3/25/2015

Sunrui Marine Environment Engineering Co., Ltd.	2/3/2015
Trojan Marinex	4/28/2014
Wartsila Senitec AB	4/17/2014
Wuxi Brightsky Electronic Co.	4/29/201

Infographics 8: List of LOI's Approved Vendors according to IMO

Significance of Ballast Water Management Treatment Code

As we've seen with the rest of the statistics, data, reviews, and research conducted by government agencies, non-government organizations, and private sectors all around the world, ballast water impose a serious threat to the marine ecosystem, economy, human health, and biodiversity. These factors are considered to implement the Ballast Water Management System at the BWM Convention and other workshops in relation.

The regulations and plans provided by BWMS are necessary for prescribing ballast water management practices and standard operating procedures and training. An article published by USCG said that since 2015, there has been a dramatic increase in the volume of ballast water being treated before it unloads cargo to another port, clear progress and major impact with the reduction ballast water on ships.

Economy

Implementing the regulations and following the proper management plan creates positive effects necessary for the economy as the method is more reliable, safer, and does not negatively affect the transportation process of the cargo load.

"This is a truly significant milestone for the health of our planet. The spread of invasive species has been recognized as one of the greatest threats to the ecological and economic well-being of the planet. These species are causing enormous damage to biodiversity and the valuable natural riches of the earth upon which we depend. Invasive species also cause direct and indirect health effects and the damage to the environment is often irreversible. The entry into force of the Ballast Water Management Convention will not only minimize the risk of invasions by alien species via ballast water, it will also provide a global level playing field for international shipping, providing clear and robust standards for the management of ballast water on ships."

Kitach Lim, Secretary General of the International Maritime Organization

The global and local savings are affected greatly in a positive way since the process of exchanging and treating ballast water far away from the shore is a lot cheaper and cost-efficient.

This would also practice cargo vessels and their respective companies and countries to follow certain plans and regulations imposed. This would give them the discipline and responsibility as a concerned citizen for better transportation and transactions in the future.

Environmental preservation

BWM helps to maintain and preserve native aquatic life protecting them from non-native species. It helps in minimizing and eliminating risks associated with the introduction of IAS such as spreading bacterias and unhealthy organisms within the territorial waters and disrupting the ecosystem and biodiversity as a whole.

This also helps in decreasing the effects on fishing, sea farming, and deterioration to port facilities.

Human Health

All the negative effects imposed by IAS such as tolerating foul-odor, accumulation of bacterias which could bring diseases, decreasing the number of relevant species and organisms, and connection between the marine area to the environment that greatly affects us individuals are prevented, controlled, and eliminated.

A healthy ecosystem is maintained by a balance through different limiting and environmental factors such as geography, food availability, presence and absence of predators, nature, and thereof. A sudden visit from an Invasive species would bring major change. Regardless of where they came from, how they arrive, and where would their new expected homes would be, they still put the economy, environment, public health, and ecosystems at risk!

The Invasive Species whether aquatic or not are the result of millennia of co-evolution by organisms adapting to the environment of one are to another. If the limiting factors of a habitat fail to stop the growth of species, then it would multiply, out-competing native species, bringing billions of dollars and irreparable change and damage to biodiversity.

The proper training for the ships' crew and administration should involve awareness of the ecological and health hazards posed by the loading and unloading of ballast water and maintaining tanks and equipment free from sediment. On the other hand, the United Nations Conference on Environment and Development (UNCED) that was held in Rio de Janeiro in 1992 recognized the issue as a major international concern.

The 18th session of the IMO Assembly in 1993 adopted a resolution A.774 (18) based on the 1991 guidelines requesting the MEPC and MSC to research their studies in order to further develop internationally applicable legal provisions. The ICES WGITMO also emphasizes the need to follow this resolution. This year as well, it was also suggested to exchange ballast water to the seawater to minimize the risks of biodiversity and economic hazards.

Other Multilateral Environmental Agency (MEAs) such as the United Nations Convention on the Law of the Sea (UNCLOS) and the Convention on Biological Diversity (CBD) support IMO's effort in prevention, managing, and controlling alien species.

There are plenty more of positive impacts of the BWMS with the marine organisms and species, to the public, to the economic state of a country, business growth, and the planet. It is important to note that each holds a responsibility to contribute to the protection of our marine and coastal environment because we are living in the same environment, whether we are part of an organization or just an individual, which was affected by the threats imposed by ballast water. Once affected by invasive marine species, the effects are now irreversible.

***

List of Abbreviations and Acronyms

(alphabetical order according to abb/arr)

A
Australian Quarantine and Inspection Service **(AQIS).**

B
Ballast Water Exchange **(BWE)**
Ballast Water Management Plan **(BWMP)**
International Convention for the Control and Management of Ships' Ballast Water and Sediments **(BWM Convention)**
Ballast Water Management System Code **(BWMS Code)**

C
Compound Annual Growth Rate **(CAGR)**
Convention on Biological Diversity **(CBD)**
Clean Water Act **(CWA)**

E
Exclusive Economic Zone **(EEZ)**
Environment Protection Authority **(EPA)**

G
Gross Domestic Product **(GDP)**
Global Environment Facility **(GEF)**

I
Invasive Aquatic Species **(IAS)**
International Council for the Exploration of the Sea **(ICES)**
International Maritime Organization **(IMO)**
Internal Revenue Service **(IRS)**

L

Liquefied Natural Gas **(LNG)**
Letter of Intent **(LOI)**

M

Multilateral Environmental Agency **(MEAs)**
Marine Environmental Protection Committee **(MEPC)**

N

Nonindigenous Aquatic Nuisance and Prevention and
Control Act of 1990 **(NANPCA)**
National System for the Prevention and Management
of Marine Pest Incursions **(National System)**
National Economic Assessment **(NEA)**
National Invasive Species Information Center **(NISIC)**
National Monitoring Strategy **(NMS)**
National Pollutant Discharge Elimination System
(NPDES).

P

Partnering Countries **(PCs).**
Photovoltaic **(PV)**

S

International Convention for the Safety of Life at Sea
(SOLAS)

T

Total Enterprise Value **(TEV)**

U

United Nations **(UN)**
United Nations Conference on Environment and
Development **(UNCED)**

United Nations Convention on the Law of the Sea
(UNCLOS)
United Nations Development Program **(UNDP)**

W
World Health Organization **(WHO)**

***

Index

Advent - the appearance of an important or notable person; the arrival of cargo vessels in coastline.
Annulled - to declare an official agreement invalid.
Approximately - used to indicate a stated number, amount, or value into something almost, exactly, and not completely.
Ballasting - to give stability to a ship by loading heavy cargo loads either in the form of solid rocks or ballast water.
Ballast Water - a water ballast complacent to a cargo load with negative impact to the environment, ecological and biodiversity hazard, and public health.
Biodiversity - a complex term that is compromised everything around the world such as the genes, species, creatures, and the entire ecosystem.
Coastline - also called as the seashore; an area where the land and ocean meets.
Compensation - rewarding or replacing something that was missing or removed.
Dilution - a process where the particles of a solute is

decreasing through mixing solvents.

Extinction - a situation where an organism or material does no longer exist.

Hydraulic - a technology applied using Science and Engineering involving mechanical properties and liquid.

International Trade - the exchange of products from one country (or place) to one another; exporting and importing cargo load.

Invasive species - an organism or exotic species that was introduced accidentally, forcefully, or deliberately from a location that is not part of their natural habitat and bringing negative effects towards it.

Latitude - a geographic coordinate system that has an angular distance north or south.

Legislation - also known as the law, implemented by the Governing Body in Power and Government.

Longatational - a geographic coordinate system that has position on a surface of the earth pointing to the west and east.

Nautical miles - a unit of measurement used to calculate the distances at sea or territorial waters.

Offshore - ship or vessel moving away from the shore.

Portside - coastal term describing the left part of the ship.

Prolific - also termed as plentiful; present in large numbers or quantities.

Shipboard - coastal term describing the right part of the ship.

Shoreline - a part in ocean where bodies of water meets.

Tonnage - a measurement in merchant or cargo ship.

Vessel - simply a ship or a large boat; a container that holds the liquid.

Voyage - a long journey in the bodies of water.
Bibliography

Ballast Water

- *Clear Seas Center - Article*
  https://clearseas.org/en/blog/importance-bal
  last-water-management/

- *North American Fishing Channel - Video*

https://www.youtube.com/watch?v=KYIJdhw8NcA

- *Environment Protection Authority Victoria*
  https://www.epa.vic.gov.au/ and
  https://www.epa.vic.gov.au/your-environ
  ment/water/ballast-water

- *European Maritime Safety Agency (EMSA)*
  http://www.emsa.europa.eu/implementat
  ion-tasks/environment/ballast-water.html

History

- *WMU Journal of Maritime Affairs - Maritime
  safety and the ISM code: A Study of
  Investigated Casualties and Incidents*
  https://link.springer.com/article/10.1007/
  s13437-013-0051-8

- *Brill: Toward an Effective Ballast Water
  Legislative and Implementation Regime:
  Lessons for Ghana*
  https://brill.com/view/journals/ocyo/28/1/
  article-p526_19.xml?crawler=true

- *Entengineers - Research and Statistics* https://www.edtengineers.com/blog-post/ballast-water-management-history-application-and-legislation

Ballast Water Management Convention (BWM Convention)

- *Coastal Wiki - Article* http://www.coastalwiki.org/wiki/Ballast_water

- International Convention for the Control and Management of Ships' Ballast Water and Sediments (BWM) http://www.imo.org/en/About/Conventions/ListOfConventions/Pages/International-Convention-for-the-Control-and-Management-of-Ships'-Ballast-Water-and-Sediments-(BWM).aspx

- IMO Frequently Asked Questions Implementing the Ballast Water Management Convention http://www.imo.org/en/MediaCentre/HotTopics/Documents/FAQ%20-%20Implementing%20the%20Ballast%20Water%20Management%20Convention.pdf

- *Seagull Maritime - Article* https://www.seagull.no/newsroom/stories/ArtMID/1039/ArticleID/159/BWM-Code-What-are-the-training-requirements

- *International Maritime Organization - Ballast Water Management* http://www.imo.org/en/OurWork/Environ

ment/BallastWaterManagement/Pages/
Default.aspx

- *Comparative study of approved IMO
  technologies for treatment of ballast waters*
  https://upcommons.upc.edu/bitstream/h
  andle/2117/123231/136380_TFM%20E
  DUARDO%20SAENZ%20ALCANTARA.
  pdf?sequence=1&isAllowed=y

- Brighthubengineering: Ballast Water
  Management Plans and Different Methods
  of Ballast Water Exchange
  https://www.brighthubengineering.com/
  marine-history/63157-ballast-water-man
  agement/

Ballast Water Tanks

- *Wartsila - Article*
  https://www.wartsila.com/encyclopedia/t
  erm/ballast-water-exchange-at-sea

- *Marine Online - Video*
  https://www.youtube.com/watch?v=9g89
  KEbYd6I

- *National Oceanic and Atmospheric
  Administration US Department of
  Commerce*
  https://oceanservice.noaa.gov/facts/port
  -starboard.html

- *Bright Hub Engineering - Article*
  https://www.brighthubengineering.com/n
  aval-architecture/66722-what-is-ballast-

> water

- *Marine Insight - Article*
  https://www.marineinsight.com/naval-arc
  hitecture/a-guide-to-ballast-tanks-on-shi
  ps/

- *Bulk Carrier Guide*
  http://bulkcarrierguide.com/structural-co
  nfiguration-ballast-tanks.html

Negative Effects of IAS:

- Coastal Management: Ballast Water Risk
  Indication for the North Sea
  https://www.tandfonline.com/doi/full/10.1
  080/08920753.2016.1233794

- GloBallast Partnership Economic
  Assessment of Ballast Water Management:
  A Synthesis of the National Assessments
  conducted by the Lead Partnering Countries
  of the GEF-UNDP-IMO GloBallast
  Partnerships Programme
  http://www.imo.org/en/OurWork/Environ
  ment/MajorProjects/Documents/Mono24
  _English.pdf

Invasive Aquatic Species:

- *International Maritime Organization - 10
  Major IAS*
  http://www.imo.org/en/OurWork/Environ
  ment/BallastWaterManagement/Pages/
  AquaticInvasiveSpecies(AIS).aspx

- *Smithsonian Ocean - Article*
  https://ocean.si.edu/ocean-life/5-invasiv

e-species-you-should-know

- *Zebra Mussels*
  https://www.usgs.gov/faqs/what-are-zeb
  ra-mussels-and-why-should-we-care-ab
  out-them?qt-news_science_products=0
  #qt-news_science_products and
  https://www.fws.gov/fisheries/ANS/index
  .html and
  https://www.lakegeorgeassociation.org/e
  ducate/science/lake-george-invasive-sp
  ecies/zebra-mussel/

- *Green Crabs*
  https://nas.er.usgs.gov/queries/factsheet
  .aspx?SpeciesID=190 and
  http://www.dfo-mpo.gc.ca/species-espec
  es/profiles-profils/europeangreencrab-cr
  abevert-eng.html

- Cholera
  https://emedicine.medscape.com/article/
  962643-overview

- Cladocera (Water Fleas)
  https://www.encyclopedia.com/environm
  ent/encyclopedias-almanacs-transcripts-
  and-maps/cladocera-water-fleas

Ballast Cycle:
- *International Maritime Organization - Ballast
  Tanks Article*
  http://www.imo.org/en/MediaCentre/Hot
  Topics/BWM/Pages/default.aspx

- *Maritime Online - Ballast Water and Cycle Video*
  https://www.youtube.com/watch?v=Sr2nCvOdGvE&t=316s

BWM Treatment System:

- *Marine Online - Video*
  https://www.youtube.com/watch?v=9g89KEbYd6I

- *Marine Insight - Article*
  https://www.marineinsight.com/naval-architecture/different-technologies-for-ballast-water-treatmenand
  https://www.marineinsight.com/tech/how-ballast-water-treatment-system-works/

- IRL Class: A GUIDE TO BALLAST WATER MANAGEMENT

http://www.irclass.org/media/2449/bwm_booklet.pdf

Legislation of GloBallast in Other Countries

- *Ballast Water: Extremely Convenient for the Shipping Industry but Disastrous for Coastal Waters and the Environment: A Study on the Effect of Ballast Water on Various Coasts and the Laws and Regulations in Place Regarding Ballast Water*
  https://pdfs.semanticscholar.org/da69/e16a67e8dcfdfe0eae3f1313688d498e5ec1.pdf

Vendor Lists

- *Technavio: Global Ballast Water Management Market 2019-2023* https://www.technavio.com/report/global-ballast-water-management-market-industry-analysis

- *Fathom World - Article* https://fathom.world/top-5-vendors-global-ballast-water-management-market/

- *Business Wire: A Berkshire Hathaway Company - Article* https://www.businesswire.com/news/home/20170725005722/en/Top-5-Vendors-Global-Ballast-Water-Management

- *Safety4Sea - Article* https://safety4sea.com/list-of-manufacturers-pursuing-bwts/

- *AlfaLava PureBallast* https://www.alfalaval.com/microsites/pureballast/

- *GEA BallastMaster UltraV BWTS* https://www.gea.com/en/products/ballastmaster-ultraV.jsp

- *Veola Water Technologies* https://www.veoliawatertechnologies.com/en/about-us

GloBallast - Cost Discharge per country
- Economic Assessment of Ballast Water

Management
http://www.imo.org/en/OurWork/Environment/MajorProjects/Documents/Mono24_English.pdf